Common Core Le
Rocks an

MW00912824

By Car
Published by Gallopade International, Inc.
©Carole Marsh/Gallopade
Printed in the U.S.A. (Peachtree City, Georgia)

TABLE OF CONTENTS

G: Includes Graphic Organizer

GO: Graphic Organizer is also available 8½" x 11" online
download at www.gallopade.com/client/go
(numbers above correspond to the graphic organizer numbers online)

What Are Minerals?

Read the text and answer the questions.

Minerals are naturally occurring, inorganic materials that have definite physical and chemical properties. A mineral always has the same chemical and physical properties. Therefore, geologists can classify minerals by their chemical and physical properties. Minerals are also usually solid and have a crystal structure. This means the atoms that compose minerals have an orderly, repeated pattern. Physical properties of minerals include hardness, luster, color and several other descriptive characteristics.

Minerals are made of nonliving matter called chemical elements. A chemical element is a substance that cannot be broken into any simpler substance. Chemical elements are the building blocks of all minerals. Sometimes a mineral is made up of just one chemical element. Most of the time, however, a mineral is a combination of two or more chemical elements.

Salt, for example, is a combination of the chemical elements sodium and chlorine. When chemically joined, sodium and chlorine form salt crystals. Salt occurs naturally—you can find it in the ocean or in large chunks of "rock salt" formed by the Earth. It has a white color and low luster, and it is relatively soft. It also has a very strong flavor!

1. A. Use the text to define minerals and chemical elements.
    B. Explain why chemical elements are the "building blocks" of minerals. Cite evidence from the text to support your answer.

2. A. Identify at least three physical properties of minerals
    B. Describe at least three physical properties of salt.

3. Match the following questions to whether they are best answered by paragraph 1, 2, or 3 of the text.
    A. _____How do scientists classify minerals?
    B. _____What are minerals made of?
    C. _____What are minerals?

4. What properties do scientists use to classify minerals? Why?

Properties of Minerals

Read the text and answer the questions.

Minerals can be identified and described based on their properties.

Color is one of the most common ways to describe minerals. However, it is not always the best way. A single mineral may appear in a variety of colors. Also, a mineral can tarnish or oxidize, meaning its color can change when its surface is exposed to moisture and air. The intensity of color can be dark, very dark, light, pale, deep, dull, shiny, or bright. Adjectives like streaked, splotchy, mottled, speckled, layered, or banded are ways to describe the distribution of color in a mineral.

Luster is the way a mineral reflects light. Minerals can be described as metallic (gold, bronze, copper, and silver), pearly, glassy, silky, greasy, brilliant, or dull.

Cleavage is when certain minerals break in a definite way. For example, mica cleaves (breaks) into thin sheets, galena cleaves into little cubes, and feldspar cleaves into little steps.

Streak is the color of powder left when a mineral is scraped across a hard, rough surface like a bathroom tile. It is not unusual for minerals of one color to leave streaks of a different color.

Specific gravity of a mineral is its relative weight compared to the weight of an equal volume of water. Specific gravity determines the density of the mineral.

---

1. A. What is the disadvantage of using color to identify minerals?
   B. What can you infer about the use of color as a way to describe minerals based on the color-descriptive adjectives listed in the text?
   C. What is the relationship between a mineral's color and its streak?

2. What can you infer about the luster of a metallic mineral?

3. How would you test the cleavage of a mineral?

4. What is the relationship between specific gravity and density?

5. Use an online resource to identify three different minerals. Organize the photographs in a visual presentation, and identify the properties of each mineral. Share your presentation with your class.

Common Minerals

Read the text and answer the questions.

There are more than 4,000 types of minerals. Only about 30 minerals, however, are commonly found in the Earth's crust.

Quartz is the most common mineral found in rocks. In its crystalized form, quartz is used as a gemstone in jewelry. Varieties of quartz include amethyst, citrine, and rose quartz. Quartz is used in manufacturing glass and paints. Feldspar is another common rock-forming mineral. About 60% of the Earth's crust is made of feldspar. People use feldspar to make glass and pottery.

Diamond is the hardest natural mineral. A hard mineral can scratch a softer mineral, but a softer mineral cannot scratch a harder mineral. Because of their hardness, diamonds are often used for cutting metal and polishing other minerals. Because of their high luster, diamonds are used in jewelry. In contrast, talc is the softest mineral. It is so soft, it can be scratched with your fingernail. Talc is dull and powdery, and it is commonly used in baby powder.

Many <u>metals</u>, or ores, are minerals as well. Aluminum is the most abundant metal element in the Earth's crust. It is used in buildings, machinery, and packaging. Iron is a common mineral known for its strength. People use iron for making tools and building houses.

1. List four common minerals found in the Earth's crust.

2. "Only about 30 minerals are commonly found in the Earth's crust." Make at least three inferences about the other 3,970+ minerals.

3. Can feldspar scratch a diamond? Why or why not?

4. Describe the organizational style of this text. How are paragraphs 2-4 similar? Which one of these three paragraphs is the most different from the others? Explain why.

5. A. Use the text to give a synonym for <u>metals</u>.
   B. Are all metals minerals? Are all minerals metals?

6. Write a short journal entry identifying some of the minerals you use in your everyday life and explain how they benefit you.

Crystal Structure

Read the text, look at the photographs, and answer the questions.

> Minerals have a crystal structure. In a crystal, atoms or molecules join together in a pattern that repeats itself over and over to create a certain shape. The pattern can be simple or complex. The resulting shape may be a cube, a prism, cylindrical, or some other distinct shape. For example, a sugar crystal forms in a six-sided prism, often with more rounded edges. Salt crystals form in nearly perfect cubes with six sides and sharp edges. Many crystals grow large because the easiest way for a new crystal to grow is to attach itself to an older crystal.

Courtesy of Wikimedia Commons

1. Use the text to label each photograph as either sugar or salt.

2. Compare and contrast sugar and salt crystals.

3. Compare and contrast the luster of sugar and salt.

4. What qualities of sugar and salt make them useful for cooking?

5. What properties of sugar and salt are you NOT able to identify using the photographs?

6. In your opinion, what is the easiest way to tell sugar from salt?

Testing Mineral Hardness

Read the texts and answer the questions.

> Hardness is one of the properties that can be used to describe and identify minerals. The hardness of a mineral is its ability to resist scratching.
>
> Friedrich Mohs was a German scientist who studied minerals. More than 100 years ago, he developed a hardness scale. The Mohs Scale of Hardness is used to describe the hardness of minerals using numbers. Any mineral's hardness can be determined by attempting to scratch it with the index minerals listed in the scale.
>
> Talc is the softest mineral. It has a hardness of 1 on the scale. Diamond is the hardest mineral, and it has a hardness of 10.

1. What is the purpose of the Mohs Scale of Hardness?

2. If quartz scratches gypsum, what can you infer about quartz and what can you infer about gypsum?

3. Identify the hardness for the 10 index minerals in the Mohs Scale of Hardness. Write each mineral on the chart beside its corresponding hardness number. First use the text above to add talc and diamond to the chart. Then use the information in the "What Scratches What" box to correctly add the other 8 minerals to the chart.

What Scratches What?

- Everything scratches calcite, except gypsum and talc.

- Fluorite scratches gypsum and calcite but not apatite.

- Corundum scratches everything except diamonds.

- Feldspar scratches apatite, and quartz scratches feldspar.

* Topaz scratches quartz but not corundum.

Mohs Scale of Hardness

Hardness	Index Mineral
1	
2	
3	
4	
5	
6	
7	
8	
9	
10	

Useful Minerals

Use online resources to research how people use minerals. Then complete the graphic organizer by identifying several minerals and explaining their usefulness.

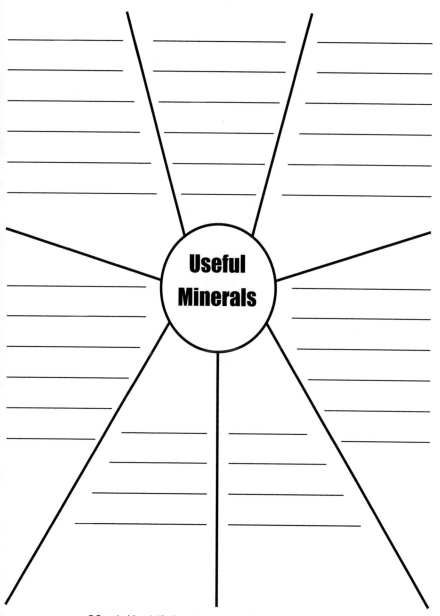

Useful Minerals

What Are Rocks?

Read the text and answer the questions.

> Rocks are everywhere. The Earth's crust is made up of rock. Mountains, canyons and riverbeds are all made of rocks. The gravel in a driveway and the sand on the beach are rocks as well.
>
> What are rocks? Rocks are solids that occur naturally and are made of two or more minerals. For example, granite is a type of rock made from the minerals feldspar, quartz, and mica.
>
> Rocks on the Earth are always changing over time. Rocks form, break down, form again, change, break down, form again, and continuously change in a process known as the <u>rock cycle</u>.
>
> Rocks are formed through geological processes, and depending on how they are formed, they are classified as igneous, sedimentary, or metamorphic.

1. Use the text to explain the difference between rocks and minerals.

2. A. What are the three main types of rocks?
   B. How are rocks classified into one of these three types?

3. Use the text to define <u>rock cycle</u>.

4. Complete the graphic organizer by identifying the main idea of the text and several supporting details.

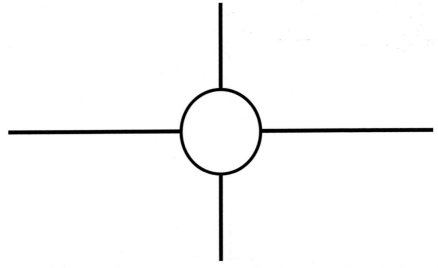

Rock Poetry

Read the poem and answer the questions.

Rocks

Three types of rock,
Are a must,
These types of rocks,
Make Earth's crust...

Igneous rocks,
When lava halts,
Are volcanic rocks,
Like basalts...

Sedimentary rocks,
Should it be known,
Compressed like coal,
Or limestone...

Metamorphic rock
Made by change,
Of temp and pressure
Run a range...

4 billion years?
Rock's been here!
I don't think,
They'll disappear!

1. Describe the style of this poem. Is it formal, informal, scientific, descriptive, informative, etc.?

2. Make a comprehensive list of facts that you can identify or infer from this poem.

3. Do you agree or disagree with the last stanza about the future of rocks? Why or why not?

4. For each of the following questions, you will need to make inferences and make an educated guess. As you answer each question, also explain your reasoning.
   A. What inferences would you make about the author of the poem?
   B. What was the author's purpose in writing the poem?
   C. Who do you think the author expected to read the poem?
   D. How might the author get the poem to his or her audience?

Three Types of Rocks

Read the text and answer the questions.

There are billions upon billions of rocks on the Earth! Yet, each rock falls into one of three groups: igneous, sedimentary, and metamorphic. Which group a rock belongs to depends on how the rock was formed.

Igneous rocks form when molten lava (magma) erupts from a volcano, cools, and turns to solid rock. Igneous rocks form with lots of fire and heat.

Sedimentary rocks form when layers of sand, clay, and bits of rock are pressed together over a long period of time. Sedimentary rocks are often pressed flat with visible layers. Often, these layers contain fossils.

Metamorphic rocks form when igneous or sedimentary rocks are changed by extreme heat and pressure due to the movement of the Earth's crust. Metamorphic rocks form deep within the Earth.

1. A. How do <u>igneous rocks</u> form?
    B. How do <u>sedimentary rocks</u> form?
    C. How do <u>metamorphic rocks</u> form?

2. Where do you think you would most likely see each of these types of rocks? Use logical reasoning to support your answer.

3. What characteristics make sedimentary rock easy to identify?

4. What is the effect of heat and pressure upon sedimentary rock?

5. A. Choose a type of rock. Next, write a story about your rock from the rock's point of view. Do not mention the name of your rock. Include facts about how it formed, where it formed, and how long it took to form. Your story could also include facts about what minerals it is made of, what it looks like, and what its future might be!
    B. Proofread, edit, and revise your work.
    C. Read your story to your class. Could your audience accurately identify your type of rock?

Three Types of Rocks

Complete the graphic organizer by comparing and contrasting igneous, sedimentary, and metamorphic rock.

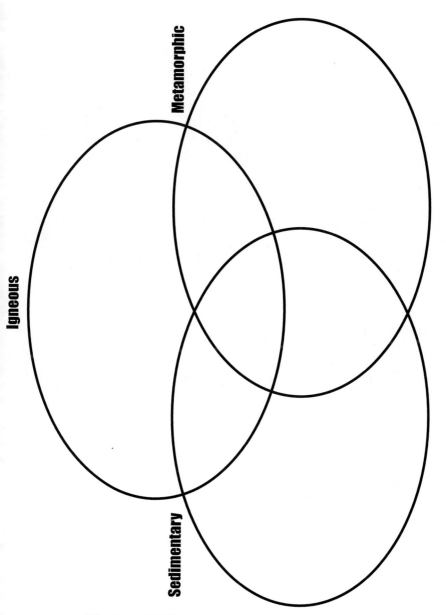

Name that Rock!

Use what you know and an online resource to identify the rocks in the photographs as igneous, sedimentary, or metamorphic, and write the name of each rock in the chart under the correct heading.

Conglomerate

Gneiss

Basalt

Limestone

Marble

Grabbo

Sandstone

Quartzite

Granite

Shale

Slate

Obsidian

Igneous	Sedimentary	Metamorphic

Let's Dig Deeper: Igneous Rocks

Read the text and answer the questions.

Igneous comes from the Greek word for *fire*. Igneous rock is formed by fire and heat. Deep inside the Earth is very hot. Minerals there melt into a liquid, called magma. As magma is pushed up toward the Earth's surface, it cools and becomes solid igneous rock.

Not all igneous rocks look the same. That is because they cool in different ways. Sometimes magma cools slowly underneath the Earth's surface. The rocks that form from this slow cooling are called intrusive igneous rocks. The slow-cooling process causes these rocks to form large crystals. Granite is an example of an intrusive igneous rock.

Other igneous rocks form when volcanoes erupt and magma spews out from the volcano. When magma reaches the surface of the Earth, it is called lava. Lava cools quickly and forms rocks with small crystals. These rocks are called extrusive igneous rocks. Basalt is an example of an extrusive igneous rock, as is obsidian. In fact, obsidian cools so fast that it has no crystals. It looks like shiny, black glass instead of a rock!

Pumice is an unusual lightweight extrusive rock formed when lava explodes out of a violent volcano. Bubbles form as the lava quickly loses pressure and cools at the same time. Pumice rock is so light it can float in water!

1. A. What are the two classifications of igneous rocks?
    B. How is their formation similar?
    C. What are the two main distinctions between them?

2. A. What effect does slow cooling have on igneous rock?
    B. What effect does fast cooling have on igneous rock?

3. Compare and contrast the physical properties of intrusive igneous rocks and extrusive igneous rocks.

4. Use the text to compare and contrast obsidian and pumice.

Let's Dig Deeper: Sedimentary Rocks

Read the text and look at the diagram. Then answer the questions.

> Sedimentary rocks usually form from layers of sediment deposited at the bottom of lakes, rivers, and oceans. Sedimentary rocks come in a variety of colors, and layers of different colors are often visible within a single rock. Fossils of organisms trapped as the rock was forming are often found between the layers.
>
> Limestone is a sedimentary rock formed from tiny pieces of shells of dead, sea animals that have been cemented together. Sandstone is a sedimentary rock formed from grains of sand pressed together. Conglomerate is a sedimentary rock formed from sand and rounded pebbles. Shale is formed from mud and clay.

1. Wind, water, and ice constantly break up rocks into smaller pieces. This is called erosion.

2. The small rock pieces, which include pebbles, gravel, sand, and clay, are transported to new locations through rivers and ocean currents, erosion, and wind.

4. Over time, the sediments are either pressed or cemented together to form a rock. The rock formed is called sedimentary rock.

3. The small rock pieces, along with pieces of shell, plants, and animal remains, are called sediments. Sediments are deposited in lakes and oceans, and on land, where they settle and pile up in flat layers.

1. Give three examples of weathering.

2. Explain how sedimentary rocks got their name.

3. Explain how a fossil gets formed inside a sedimentary rock.

4. Number these four steps in the order they occur:

   _____cementation or compaction   _____deposition
   _____transportation   _____weathering

5. Make inferences to describe differences between a sedimentary rock that is "pressed" together and one that is "cemented" together.

Let's Dig Deeper: Metamorphic Rocks

Read the text and answer the questions.

Metamorphic rocks are sedimentary and igneous rocks that have been changed by heat and pressure. Metamorphic comes from Greek words meaning *change* and *form*. Metamorphic rocks are the least common of the three types of rock.

Metamorphic rocks form deep inside the Earth. Here, the Earth is very hot. The heat comes from the magma in the Earth. Here, there is also great pressure. The pressure comes from layers of rocks piled on top of layers and layers of rock. All of this heating and squeezing for several million years can change one type of rock into another type of rock. For example, sandstone becomes quartzite, shale becomes slate, and limestone becomes marble.

Foliated metamorphic rocks are rocks that have layers, or visible bands. Schist is the most common metamorphic rock. It consists of layers of different minerals and can be split into thin, irregular plates. Non-foliated metamorphic rocks, such as marble, are not layered.

1. What three "things" are required in order to change sedimentary and igneous rock into metamorphic rock?

2. Describe the difference between a foliated and a non-foliated metamorphic rock.

3. Explain why metamorphic rocks rarely contain fossils.

4. Write a hypothesis to explain why metamorphic rock is the least common of the three types of rock.

5. A. Use an online resource to compile photographs of at least five different kinds of metamorphic rocks.
   B. Compare and contrast the physical properties of the rocks.
   C. List any common characteristics, interesting observations, or themes you have identified about metamorphic rocks.
   D. Create a digital presentation to show each rock and describe its physical properties.
   E. Share your presentation with your class.

Rock Cycle

In small groups, use what you know about the rock cycle and the three types of rock to complete steps of the rock cycle in the graphic organizer. Then answer the questions.

> Rocks are constantly being recycled! On the Earth, rocks erode and are formed over and over again into different rocks. Of course, this takes millions of years! It's called the rock cycle.

1. What part does igneous rock play in the rock cycle?

2. What part does sedimentary rock play in the rock cycle?

3. What part does metamorphic rock play in the rock cycle?

Rock Cycle

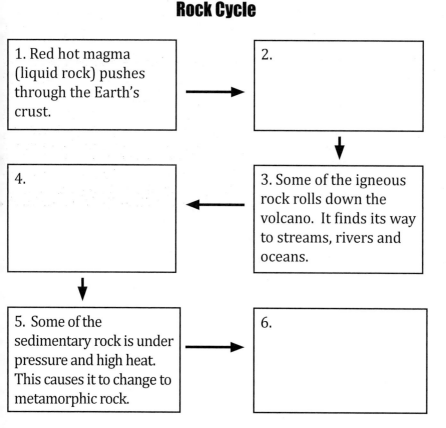

1. Red hot magma (liquid rock) pushes through the Earth's crust.

2.

3. Some of the igneous rock rolls down the volcano. It finds its way to streams, rivers and oceans.

4.

5. Some of the sedimentary rock is under pressure and high heat. This causes it to change to metamorphic rock.

6.

Let's Explore a Cave!

Read the text and answer the questions.

Caves are natural openings into the Earth. They are usually dark and often very deep. They are found in many types of rock, but they are most common in limestone, dolomite, and gypsum.

Thousands of caves twist and turn beneath the Earth's surface. No one knows the exact number of caves, but Tennessee has more than 9,500 caves and Missouri has over 6,000. Caves exist all over the world. They come in many sizes and shapes. Some caves have an entrance at the Earth's surface. Others do not. Some caves are filled with air while other caves are filled with water. Caves often contain sand, mud, clay, silt, or other sediment.

It takes millions of years for most caves to form. The way a cave forms determines what type of cave it is. The largest and most common type of cave is a solution cave. Other types of caves are sea caves, lava caves, and glacier caves.

Cave environments are often fragile and can easily be destroyed when light, air, bacteria and people enter their chambers. Caves can have rare plants and animals living in them. Caves also have very distinctive mineral formations, fossils, and artifacts. For scientists who study the Earth's history, caves often reveal deep layers of sedimentary rock. These layers of sedimentary rock give clues to calculating the Earth's age and to identifying plants and animals that lived long ago.

1. A. What do all caves have in common?
   B. How are some caves different from others?

2. Spelunkers are people who like to explore caves. Work with a partner and make a list of good rules for spelunkers. Think about what safety precautions they should take, what tools they should bring, and what they should or should not do when inside a cave. Use the text to help give you ideas. Explain why you made the rules you made.

3. Explain what information can be gathered from caves and how.

4. Research one of the types of caves (solution, lava, sea, or glacier). Organize your information into a visual presentation. Be creative. Give your presentation to your class.

Spelunker Journal

Write a spelunker journal entry.

Just a short drive from almost anywhere is a cave waiting to be explored! Caving, also known as spelunking, is the exploration of caves as a hobby. People who like to explore caves are called spelunkers, or cavers. Spelunkers often keep journals of their spelunking adventures.

Pretend you are a spelunker. Write a journal entry for your exploration of a solution cave. What kind of gear did you need to take with you and why? What type of clothes did you wear? Why? Describe the cave and the different rock formations you encountered. What types of rocks did you see and how did you identify them? Did you see any rare plants or animals? What were your emotions as you explored the cave?

Stalactites & Stalagmites

Read the text and answer the questions.

Stalactites and stalagmites are two rock formations found in caves around the world. Stalactites often look like rocky spikes hanging from the ceiling while stalagmites often look like cones growing from the ground.

Stalactites and stalagmites are formed by mineral-rich water that seeps through the ground from above. As water drips from the ceiling of a cave, it deposits minerals on the rock. Over time, a stalactite forms where the water drips from the ceiling. These minerals continue to pile up, building the stalactite closer and closer to the ground. The color of the mineral that is deposited will determine the color of the stalactite.

What happens when the water hits the cave floor? The water deposits minerals there, too! As water drips from the cave's ceiling, it deposits minerals in piles that eventually grow larger and larger, forming a tower of rock called a stalagmite.

1. Use the text to label the photographs as either <u>stalactite</u> or <u>stalagmite</u>.

_____   _____

2. A. What are stalactites and stalagmites made from?
   B. Are they considered a rock or a mineral? Explain why.

3. Explain why stalactites and stalagmites can form in many colors.

Rock & Mineral Words

Use a dictionary or other resources to complete the graphic organizer for each vocabulary word.

alloy	fracture	matter
color	igneous	metamorphic
crystal	geologist	sediment
density	hardness	streak
fossil	luster	

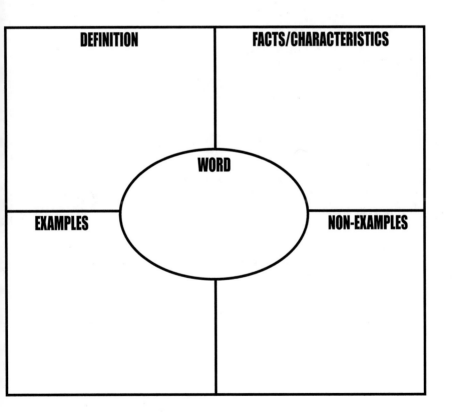

Valuable Rocks–Gems!

Read the text and answer the questions.

Gemstones are rare mineral crystals valued for their bright colors and brilliant gleam. Most gemstones are used for jewelry or decoration. When used this way, they are usually cut and polished. Many of the resulting gemstones are transparent. Some gemstones look similar to what the mineral looks like when found in nature. Others look very different.

Gems are often classified as either precious or semiprecious stones. When people talk about precious gems, they are usually referring to diamonds, rubies, sapphires, and emeralds. Sometimes, pearls (not really a mineral but still a gem) and opal are included.

A more scientific way to classify gems is based on their physical properties. Gems are made from different chemicals and minerals. Because they are made from different things, they have different physical properties. Diamonds are made from carbon. Rubies and sapphires are made from the mineral corundum. Emeralds are from the mineral beryl and amethysts are from quartz.

Some gems can be identified by their color, but color alone is not usually enough. For example, there are green garnets and green emeralds.

There is an entire branch of science that studies gems. The science is called gemology, and the scientists are gemologists. Laboratories around the world classify gems and grade their quality.

1. Why might some gems be called precious while others are called semiprecious? List several reasons this distinction might be made.

2. What is the scientific classification of gems usually based on?

3. Explain the relationship between minerals and gems.

4. What would happen if color was the only physical property used to identify gemstones? Explain.

5. Why do different gems have different physical properties?

Mining for Ore

Read the text and answer the questions.

> Many metals, or <u>ores</u>, are found in rocks. Some of the metals found in rocks are considered precious metals and some are considered more common or everyday metals. Gold and silver are examples of precious metals. Precious metal is removed from rock and then turned into jewelry, coins, or other valuable objects. Aluminum is an example of an everyday metal. These metals are often more abundant than precious metals. Everyday ore is used in construction, manufacturing, and many other industries.
>
> Ores are mined, or dug, from rocks in the Earth through a process called <u>mining</u>. Unfortunately, mining, which is often deep in the ground, can harm the natural landscape. Erosion and pollution are two common effects.

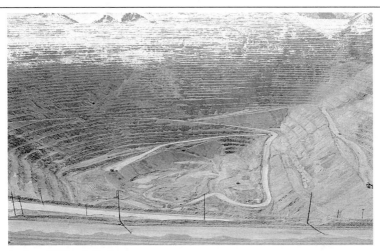

Courtesy of Wikimedia Commons

1. Use the text to define <u>ore</u> and <u>mining</u>.

2. A. Write a detailed description of the landscape in the photograph. Include what you see, and what you don't see.
    B. What can you infer about the value of ore, based on the photograph? Explain.

3. Describe the impact of mining. Use the text and the photograph to support your response.

Correlations to Common Core State Standards

For your convenience, correlations are listed page-by-page, and for the entire book!

This book is correlated to the <u>Common Core State Standards for English Language Arts</u> grades 3-8, and to <u>Common Core State Standards for Literacy in History, Science, & Technological Subjects</u> grades 6-8.

Correlations are highlighted in gray.

PAGE #	READING Includes: RI: Reading Informational Text RST: Reading Science & Technical Subjects	WRITING Includes: W: Writing WHST: Writing History/Social Studies, Science, & Technical Subjects	LANGUAGE Includes: L: Language LF: Language Foundational Skills	SPEAKING & LISTENING Includes: SL: Speaking & Listening
2	RI / RST · 1 2 3 4 5 6 7 8 9 10	W / WHST · 1 2 3 4 5 6 7 8 9 10	L / LF · 1 2 3 4 5 6	SL · 1 2 3 4 5 6
3	RI / RST · 1 2 3 4 5 6 7 8 9 10	W / WHST · 1 2 3 4 5 6 7 8 9 10	L / LF · 1 2 3 4 5 6	SL · 1 2 3 4 5 6
4	RI / RST · 1 2 3 4 5 6 7 8 9 10	W / WHST · 1 2 3 4 5 6 7 8 9 10	L / LF · 1 2 3 4 5 6	SL · 1 2 3 4 5 6
5	RI / RST · 1 2 3 4 5 6 7 8 9 10	W / WHST · 1 2 3 4 5 6 7 8 9 10	L / LF · 1 2 3 4 5 6	SL · 1 2 3 4 5 6
6	RI / RST · 1 2 3 4 5 6 7 8 9 10	W / WHST · 1 2 3 4 5 6 7 8 9 10	L / LF · 1 2 3 4 5 6	SL · 1 2 3 4 5 6
7	RI / RST · 1 2 3 4 5 6 7 8 9 10	W / WHST · 1 2 3 4 5 6 7 8 9 10	L / LF · 1 2 3 4 5 6	SL · 1 2 3 4 5 6
8	RI / RST · 1 2 3 4 5 6 7 8 9 10	W / WHST · 1 2 3 4 5 6 7 8 9 10	L / LF · 1 2 3 4 5 6	SL · 1 2 3 4 5 6
9	RI / RST · 1 2 3 4 5 6 7 8 9 10	W / WHST · 1 2 3 4 5 6 7 8 9 10	L / LF · 1 2 3 4 5 6	SL · 1 2 3 4 5 6
10	RI / RST · 1 2 3 4 5 6 7 8 9 10	W / WHST · 1 2 3 4 5 6 7 8 9 10	L / LF · 1 2 3 4 5 6	SL · 1 2 3 4 5 6
11	RI / RST · 1 2 3 4 5 6 7 8 9 10	W / WHST · 1 2 3 4 5 6 7 8 9 10	L / LF · 1 2 3 4 5 6	SL · 1 2 3 4 5 6
12	RI / RST · 1 2 3 4 5 6 7 8 9 10	W / WHST · 1 2 3 4 5 6 7 8 9 10	L / LF · 1 2 3 4 5 6	SL · 1 2 3 4 5 6
14	RI / RST · 1 2 3 4 5 6 7 8 9 10	W / WHST · 1 2 3 4 5 6 7 8 9 10	L / LF · 1 2 3 4 5 6	SL · 1 2 3 4 5 6
15	RI / RST · 1 2 3 4 5 6 7 8 9 10	W / WHST · 1 2 3 4 5 6 7 8 9 10	L / LF · 1 2 3 4 5 6	SL · 1 2 3 4 5 6
16	RI / RST · 1 2 3 4 5 6 7 8 9 10	W / WHST · 1 2 3 4 5 6 7 8 9 10	L / LF · 1 2 3 4 5 6	SL · 1 2 3 4 5 6
17	RI / RST · 1 2 3 4 5 6 7 8 9 10	W / WHST · 1 2 3 4 5 6 7 8 9 10	L / LF · 1 2 3 4 5 6	SL · 1 2 3 4 5 6
18	RI / RST · 1 2 3 4 5 6 7 8 9 10	W / WHST · 1 2 3 4 5 6 7 8 9 10	L / LF · 1 2 3 4 5 6	SL · 1 2 3 4 5 6
19	RI / RST · 1 2 3 4 5 6 7 8 9 10	W / WHST · 1 2 3 4 5 6 7 8 9 10	L / LF · 1 2 3 4 5 6	SL · 1 2 3 4 5 6
20	RI / RST · 1 2 3 4 5 6 7 8 9 10	W / WHST · 1 2 3 4 5 6 7 8 9 10	L / LF · 1 2 3 4 5 6	SL · 1 2 3 4 5 6
21	RI / RST · 1 2 3 4 5 6 7 8 9 10	W / WHST · 1 2 3 4 5 6 7 8 9 10	L / LF · 1 2 3 4 5 6	SL · 1 2 3 4 5 6
22	RI / RST · 1 2 3 4 5 6 7 8 9 10	W / WHST · 1 2 3 4 5 6 7 8 9 10	L / LF · 1 2 3 4 5 6	SL · 1 2 3 4 5 6
23	RI / RST · 1 2 3 4 5 6 7 8 9 10	W / WHST · 1 2 3 4 5 6 7 8 9 10	L / LF · 1 2 3 4 5 6	SL · 1 2 3 4 5 6
COMPLETE BOOK	RI / RST · 1 2 3 4 5 6 7 8 9 10	W / WHST · 1 2 3 4 5 6 7 8 9 10	L / LF · 1 2 3 4 5 6	SL · 1 2 3 4 5 6

For the complete Common Core standard identifier, combine your grade + "." + letter code above + "." + number code above.

In addition to the correlations indicated here, the activities may be adapted or expanded to align to additional standards and to meet the diverse needs of your unique students!

©Carole Marsh/Gallopade • www.gallopade.com • page 24